MUSCADINE

Muscadine

POEMS | **A. H. JERRIOD AVANT**

FOUR WAY BOOKS

TRIBECA

LIBRARY OF CONGRESS CATALOGING-IN-PUBLICATION DATA

Names: Avant, A. H. Jerriod, author.

Title: Muscadine : poems / A. H. Jerriod Avant.

Description: New York : Four Way Books, 2023.

Identifiers: LCCN 2023004445 (print) | LCCN 2023004446 (ebook) | ISBN 9781954245709 (trade paperback) | ISBN 9781954245716 (ebook)

Subjects: LCGFT: Poetry.

Classification: LCC PS3601.V355 M87 2023 (print) | LCC PS3601.V355 (ebook) | DDC 813/.6--dc23/eng/20230317

LC record available at https://lccn.loc.gov/2023004445

LC ebook record available at https://lccn.loc.gov/2023004446

This book is manufactured in the United States of America and printed on acid-free paper.

Four Way Books is a not-for-profi literary press. We are grateful for the assistance we receive from individual donors, public arts agencies, and private foundations including the NEA, and the New York State Council on the Arts, a state agency.

We are a proud member of the Community of Literary Magazines and Presses.

CONTENTS

Dedicated to our father, Robert Allen Avant Sr., our mother, Vernice Black Avant, our brother, Robert Allen Avant Jr., and our uncles Michael Ray Avant and Willie Gene Avant. Without your ahead-of-time blessings, love, fight and support, this book would not exist.

"To speak means to be in a position to use a certain syntax, to grasp the morphology of this or that language, but it means above all to assume a culture, to support the weight of a civilization."

FRANTZ FANON
Black Skin, White Masks

"I'm outspoken my language is broken into a slang but it's just a dialect that I select when I hang."

SPECIAL ED
"I Got It Made"

MUSCADINE

Pride

Give me memories as
slow to leave as snails.

In foreign   and perhaps
fragile years   I'll still be able

to recognize semen
and expect the smoke.

Champ's name   causes no
stress to fill the mouth.

Quieter than fear   or any
of fear's cousins. Vernice

takes nine specific pills
between spoons of grits

and long sips of an instant
coffee I love. Robert never

told us he was ill
though surely   he knew.

I've seen knowledge eat large
men alive   over a summer.

Muscadines on center
stage as the native grape.

The thick skin   the teeth
pierce   breaks to pour

sweetly across the tongue.
Look   how I hunger where

there is no hunger. Look
how Pops left   before we

thought he was done. Listen,
how the voice   of a dead man

can live. Pack me   a bag
I can fit   in my heart.

The Nerve of Death

eye red fly cheeks derivin' by spreads for pryin' meringue
a bed by weeks revivin' shy treads far tryin' abstain
fuh sked high shrieks enliven why said of fryin' a mayne

spy dread sky reeks survivin' I bred applyin' da thang
cuh shred lie reaps connivin' lye read a cryin' for pain
the dead I keeps alive in my head are dyin' again

the dead I keeps alive in my head are dyin' again
cuh shred lie reaps connivin' lye read a cryin' for pain
spy dread sky reeks survivin' I bred applyin' da thang

fuh sked high shrieks enliven why said of fryin' a mayne
a bed by weeks revivin' shy treads far tryin' abstain
eye red fly cheeks derivin' by spreads for pryin' meringue

What Deer Season Means to Me

In the house there were always two
white deep freezers packed pretty
decent with red meat. Deer season,
the hunters and the deer would satisfy
rent in season, by meat if not by cash.
It was May, I was fifteen and we smelled
fifteen or so throughout the warm insides
of the man-handled school bus, when Pops
steers quick and clear to dodge the deer
and Shirlean yells, *"I didn't even know it was
deer season."* As if deer only lived so they
could be killed during deer season.
What's a deer outside of deer season,
except a reason for deer season?

Felonious States of Adjectival Excess Featuring Comparative and Superlative Forms

my mo' favoriter   and mo' better   is my most favoritest

is mo' simpler this way   is mo' fluider   mo' wetter   most hottest

'cause the most beautifullest   is mo' beautifuller   mo' meaner

mo' flyer   and most flyest   mo' shyer   and the most shyest

is more than more intelligenter   than the panel's most ugliest

and most selectivest   is the most goodest   is the most burntest

is mo' burnter   and mo' unrulier   is the most meekest

and even mo' meeker   is the most ownablest   is mo' purchasabler

and the most purchased   thus   becomes the most purchasablest

          at the site of the most shiniest coins

my most funkiest   is also my most stolenest   but the most stolenest

can't ever be mo' funkier   than the most oldest   the most thievin'est

be the most brokest   cause the most thieved from   be the most oldest

so becomes   the most richest   who also be   the most fundedest and that makes me   the most confusedest   when I'm in the most

keptest buildings   that be   mo' kepter   than all the most

time keepin'est kats   they keep in the back   up keepin' 'em.

Mad Gas Company

at our feet lie an assemblage of split
and whole logs across a hillside of

freshly sprayed sawdust. the kill is
our installment in the tall dense series

of events we make. its purpose we feel
as much as we see the projected

silhouettes of flames on the walls.
the loggers come to steal what grows

on the land, thinking we don't value it
'cause of how it keeps. money eats at

the minds of these men. power charges
in their guts so much so they believe

what is ours, is really theirs. our arms
brim and heap with firewood for

the night. our pores brim and pour
with sweat from the day. the density

of red and white oaks ablaze could
thaw the shoulders of the coldest

muthaphuka you ever seen and now
we done made the gas company mad.

Catching

Church begins in the mouth as a hook
I cannot soothe and never saw coming

beyond this watery realm, muddy and murder-ridden,
baiting, a ritual, pierced and laid against inquisitive steel,

a fetching of the hungry, gathering of predators
to feast of the one we know loses, the one

I know wins, knows the insides of the one who loses.
The stovetop mural is a grease-splattered pool

of the ones who've gone before the one who loses,
baptized by its crackle and kiss, washing clean the

predatory soul of the one who fills me. I am
elegant-gloved for serving the one from the muddy

world of honeysuckle-laden levees and larger breeds
of itself, swimmer of lakes and rivers, grey and blue

sliver of steel, capturing me blind in sight of worm
and cricket, flickering paths just beneath the window

of the surface of the river, where the spirit breaks
its invited calm, Holy Ghost shaking off the mud

and wet of the river, backward dive into the thick
boil of June and hunger is the meal we both swallow,

all the way down to the bone, its jut and prick
against throat, the pull the teeth give to the skeleton

is a level of wanting I dare deny
in the midst of my shout and needy heave

for what sits gracefully calm
inside the bones of me.

Polistes Carolina

I avoid heat   by choosing cooler
sides of sliding glass doors. I

am as untouchable   as any ghost
cut off from the one who waits

to prove its horrific lineage and
name I reserve. The weatherwoman

reports a heat index of 105 by noon
and beyond the reaches of ample

light   thirteen or fourteen hang
and stand post outside their home

built onto our home. Hare-footed
they clutter above passageways. They

red-bodied   black-winged and deft
more precise than anything this mean

breathing   and they itch to come ruin
parts of our small   country. Inverted

they loll   in untroubled ways   and I
want to feed them flakes of their own

wings. I slide glass to neutralize the
small but fast and fiery threat. I beg

only corpses to outlast their living.
Count the screwed bodies I've

gathered   with forefingers around
the necks of toxic cannisters.

When the nest falls   I exhale until
my cheeks balloon   in relief that

I've left the nest   too wet to continue
to hang. I am the killer their house

is unable to make and I get away
with a hot throne   of shallow graves

dripping at the edges   of my feet.

The Letter Man

guilt led a man to root fuh three weeks it snowed
milk fed a land the coop but she free we blowed
quilt set a fan to scoot cuz he beat these lows

silt let a van a moot but we teach these codes
kilt wetta dan a noose fo' he sleep he chokes
built betta dan da truth but he cheap as votes

built betta dan da truth but he cheap as votes
built betta dan da loot but he sneeze he broke
kilt wetta dan a noose fo' he sleep he chokes

quilt set a fan to scoot cuz he beat these lows
milk fed a land the coop but she free we blowed
guilt led a man to root fuh three weeks it snowed

The Day a Cast of My Own Failures Rocked Me

Suppose we were there for some event
we did not want in or did. Faith flung

so hard, the cage I felt around me was
no cage, just fear, in a summer-long wither,

an idea much too small for our believin' at
the time. Suppose bendin' to kiss his cold,

thick feet will ever mean anything. How feet
of men, kissed by men, sounds biblical.

How the occasion sought to vandalize our most
underdressed prayers, which aided the gathered,

who were too heavy to be lifted and how
do you say *lift* when the moment is bent

on your fall? Suppose a god's eyes fell yellow
in your clean face, and doctors have to

stand there, helpless as you, with all those
futile books stacked in their heads; benighted

by the hour and this deteriorating conclusion.
I think it was Mother Hayes who'd started

closin' all the blinds and my first thought, "some
folk deal in metaphor subconsciously." Suppose

all this leavin' was comin' and we couldn't
brace for anything if we wanted, where

somethin' to hold onto hurries to mirage itself
into your late pseudo-rescue. Our eyes rained

salt into the dumb silence. The vitals,
a fast stage curtain, fallin', where the lead

never makes it back out to bow and there's
no encore to quell these sobbing ovations.

Unusual Tightrope

With one wrong step, the carpeted hallway floor will show
you its appetite for ankles. The creaks go unheard for the

footsteps are louder. It is a faking give, as if walking through
a hammock that won't fail. Without care for boot, heel, sandal,

sneaker, the gait, the need heading to the bedroom your
parents made love in, it can be a lonely walk. One stuffed

with memories of how when you and your dad would pass
through, you had to turn sideways so you and he could fit.

Other times, you just waited at the end for him to parade through,
just white underwear, headed to answer the front door, proudly

unashamed and huge. The photos hang in the hall, lit by
leftover light from the connecting rooms. These mementos,

pictures of grade school milestones, visits to faraway lands,
triumphs, plaques, all concluded by flowers covering the hall's

back wall. Given in sync I suppose, is a botanic rainbow offered at
his funeral, the end of a physical life filled with gusto, three-year-old

gifts that won't stop panting. I often ask what is it about hallways
that makes them seem smaller after time? My friends say, it's the

fact that your ass has grown up and because you're bigger, the
hallways get smaller. But I know that hallways don't physically

shrink the same way that grapes give up their smooth skin while
drying in the sun. And if hallways did, it'd mean they were no

different from raisins, and that my father's death somehow
brought out the sun. But there are no rays of sun, no sweeter

song here and the hallway isn't dry it just feels empty like other
tombs that miss their pharaohs. I know that perception is

real. I also feel the still air fill the hall when I'm back home as
I nearly grunt to drag myself through its groove like I'm

a corpse in a body bag of black leather. When I enter the room,
I can't help my eyes being blotted by the stack of newspapers

and magazines covering the precise two-thirds of the bed
where he'd sleep. Just enough space for my mother to

sneak under the covers after she has stayed up as absolutely
late as she could. She nods off in the front room rocking chair

to late night talk shows. I wonder if she ever takes notice of
herself. It's a long walk to wonder what fear she faces, what

fear she avoids each night without him laughing, laying next
to her. It's time-taxing for me, but I'm younger and years

quicker to step. But for her, what's the pace? Does the ghost
she might see but never share, slow or help pass the time? Am

I a body bag of sadness trying to relieve her of any hint of grief?
Does she notice it? Or when she sees any one of the three of us,

their children, is she looking for the most familiar traces of him?
I want her to find him in each give of the carpet, in every

creak of the worn flooring nailed throughout the dry hall, each
memory on both hallway walls, each petal offering oxygen to

replace the thin air. I want her to flesh him out of thin air.

Missing Person

Last time home, I saw a pair of shoes tucked into a corner
and it looked as if they hadn't been moved since he was here.

The dust on them sacred and still, when I'm home, my mind
labors in the dust. It's been six years but I say it hasn't happened.

Though the day persists, he's still tucked into a cloud tucked into
a tree in the back of a long black car and my throat won't

let my heart through no matter how flat my epiglottis falls. All about
the day breaking is clean so why this horror? A nightmare in my

wake. A black silk-blend pressed smooth, upholstering silent
emotion, boldly not a dent on him. We dare name this night

with its sun out high, hanging by its hands where the room was
too small to be holding so much ache. Our worlds now captured

by a piece of forest carved tightly, hinges now let us in or shut us out
but they fail to shut him in. A tree uprooted. The one I fell from,

and I'm the only one to find him showing up in my day. Meetings,
business trips scattered him and I knew he'd be back but not

back so soon or in this form and the way I am nervous about it
all, if I am losing it and if he's gone how is he here with me?

The dining room table, an altar where we open all bodies, either
give or take, how his form sits in cheer, naked torso and you

are to act as if his generous breasts aren't private parts. I don't
see how I see what I'm seeing. My eyes shaping a silhouette

of the man who raised me as the sun raises all of our sleepy
shadows. What gives when two realms refuse to budge

and won't make that sway completely to either world? Imagination
is a long, worn, leather belt spread around my only hope; this

yearning for Pops to adjourn a meeting he's not in, get home
to build dinner around venison; a staple holding us full. The dates

leading up, I never get wrong. Their quick succession still stings.
It seems I'm always in a reality I shouldn't be in. Somehow

our home preserves certain fingerprints. I map them and become
bored with the maps of this world. I would abandon one realm

for another when I watch him swing into the driveway and catch
his breath from the day, before exiting the vehicle. I watch him

honk the horn before he's honking it. Passes me a crisp fifty-
dollar bill because I'm there. Hands me baskets of new

pecans and muscadines we'll use. I hear him telling me how
I'm trying to split the log against the grain and how that'll

wear me out the same way lying will, the same way alcohol will my
liver and how not cleaning the yard will eat away at the lawnmower's

blades. I got a thing for fumbling through couplets. I hear him asking have I talked to Momma and he knows I have and what

I'm about to say. How I'm knocking on the window of this other realm, begging to sing my confusion until he understands me.

I'm eleven hundred and fifty-four miles from home, farther from him, and still, we continue this secret, of running into each other.

Holy Stagger

No one started to care at the smell made by the house.
Barely two bedrooms, it formed a slight square figure made

for trapping just off Indian Creek Road. Before reaching
the screen door, an odor the color of his eyes; a dingy rotting

yellow, shot staunched through the wire pores, as a curving back
is casually weakened you consider exile and the sense involved

in making all yo' breaks clean. The state got no control over
what it doesn't know it funds in this happy town where need

is relative and no one is ready to press that luck that much.
So he floods his frangible body with movements through

the same two modes made by swimming and not swimming.
Made by repeated swigs of foaming browns and clear burning

waters. Momma calls to remind him of church in the morning
so we can pick him up even though Saturday night and Sunday

morning have no distinguishable differences for him. So we still
move through this. His hands fastened to a pew in church with a

slur. The deacons let him finish because God will and none of us
be fit to play that role. The mind of a man you insist on telling,

can be a wall with a wall behind another wall. The mothers all
pity him, while I stand in this line I may not step out of.

Rocks

you're given the vehicle
to pull through curves

of a road the county
came to grade last week

and you're on your way
to grab a man to live

in your house who can't
live in his own house

whose feeding tube allows
him to eat through the

houses he lives in. you
think the full trip back

with him and forth in a
sway   wishing you were

not this nephew behind
this leather wheel. he braces

himself for violent drugs
the doctors assure will

weaken him. *it look like*
we gon get some rain today

i say   with a trail of
dust clouds and the

gravel knocking beneath
the truck. i wait for a

phrase i can make out
or a   word i can mold

a question around as
cranial nerve VIII works

to pull sentences from
mere sounds. he commits

to dialogue with a throat
filled with rocks the

oncologist say the oncologist
can't move. a piggish disease

knotted throughout his
pharynx   that don't clean

the way i've seen rocks clean
in creeks. the oto-folk make

a team of white coats you
can't get on the phone

and i don't wanna say
i don't wanna be here

no matter its truth   no
matter the sum of worry

studding these days.
i'm in too-thick-of-a-

bond with disease
treading the loose gravel

of a sharp bend   signaling
into   a difficult turn.

We Were Being Detained

before the thirty-six of us could bless the food,
he called us out of the names we resist leaving,

quick to accuse, the room of rearranging, to kill
him when no one ever begged his fall. an impulse

born in him, to drag us flat across a floor we weren't on
and we embarrass quietly. laugh and throw pillows to

save necks from the corners of coffee tables. all the
scared children, their urgent questions we wish we

could unfold for them, rattle us. i wanna vanish
from this detainment. leave only this body in the

room, where the All-Star pitcher, who "should've
made it to the league," can't control his saliva.

none of this melts down before the wads of stale
entertainment. i say to my guest, "let's just go fix

our plates together." too hungry to let him finish.
the lips in the room, too cold to be kissing. i wanted

him to stop what he wouldn't stop so bad. i wanted
to see the night zipped up again, to kill what always

happens to him, until what happens to him is cut out.

All I Eat

call my peeps my skills call my creed my bae my drawl heavy baths
sprawl dry creeks dry quills sprawl dry feed dry clay dry small petty laughs
tall try peaks try hills tall try breed try whey try gall ready calves

ball buy feast by bills ball by lead by splay buy all sweaty halves
crawl why cheat why steal crawl why speed why stay why stall steady math
all I eat I kill all I need I say I already have

all I eat I feel all I need I pray I already have
crawl why cheat why steal crawl why speed why stay why stall steady math
ball buy feast by bills ball by lead by splay buy all sweaty halves

tall try peaks try hills tall try breed try whey try gall ready calves
sprawl dry creeks dry quills sprawl dry feed dry clay dry small petty laughs
call my peeps my skills call my creed my bae my drawl heavy baths

A Triolet for Oscar Grant

If I were not a bullet I would kiss you,
Tuck your flooding flaws next to your perfections
Peel you from the concrete, leave you cool like dew.
If I were not a bullet I would kiss you,
Gift your mother with nearness, not the burden to miss you.
I would let you live well beyond my perceptions.
If I were not a bullet I would kiss you,
Tuck your flooding flaws next to your perfections.

Scared to Hold the Baby

the door wore a hopeful sign reading somebody gone was
gon "be back later." some universal late shyt. an overworked
endocrinologist claims a thirty-minute callback but don't

ever call back. laid down horny & fatigued in the bed with
its cracked clocks but not even these can drain the wild
energy from my hands. something says pull & pull & throw

these few bags of faith i have at a fat absence. i throw my
muthaphukin' hands up. plant these dead seeds in our
bedroom's wide & cold crotch, fast enough to kill time.

Animal Planet

It could've been the stiff crack
of bone or rapid gunfire
exploding bits of red in the air.

Because only for animals is it
natural to marinate for hours
in postmortem under sun.

The lions rip the gazelles
of themselves. They know
how sweet the blood is.

A Bullet on Laundry Day

Resentment wore me like a body I didn't know

wore me that way.

I held my tongue

as a scythe

attached to a mouth I didn't know

could sling a scythe that way

    sling a slice of kill so clean

     the wound got no markers,

          just a deep red flood on the skin.

Chasm so split, I hid all that fake

     red-covered forgiveness

     just out of sight, beneath my surface.

Sometimes the ones you love

you only think you love

and that secret in the way

is just a key to the door

I've all but walked through.

        Most days my heart

        is a worn-in hat

I need to clean.

Coroner in the Kitchen

after dusting off the last
cabbage, the pot drug
a warm and delicious
ghost across the house.

Corporal Punishment or How I Learned to Move Me or Let Me Go

after dodgin' my dad who be in the kitchen, i run into my mother
down the hall i run. she treats me like she's my dad. my dad sits back
and judges my horror just as my mother would if i'd gone ahead
faced my dad. i lean into the heat and thralls of country punishments.
i'm a fish on the snatched hook where others have either learned or
been warned. fed a diet of super supervision and mo' braided switches
than a boy that age of that mind would reasonably imagine. trained
to assist in facilitatin' my own torture. stripped leaves from not too
small to not too big branches twisting tight to keep the lash employed.
forged straps who listened to them show me the depths of their love
and how much it was supposed to hurt them. it was ass out and back
turned it was me helpin' momma help me and daddy showin' daddies
how to daddy. this bit to say i know it to be all reason the sharp ridges
of elm leaves still turn somersaults flying the length of my guts.

Freddie King Beatin' Eggs and It's All Love

my strut stew welts the fan a young sweet blood pops
sike the view helps to ban a tongue sweeps up sop
sly the newks dealt fuh hands o' lungs ease fuck slot

die cuz you felt a klan o' swung free mugs drop
fight fuh two belts but ran among each o'em hot
I love you betta dan a hungry hog love slop

I love you betta dan da hungriest hogs love slop
fight fuh two belts but ran among each o'em hot
die cuz you felt a klan o' swung free mugs drop

sly the newks dealt fuh hands o' lungs ease fuck slot
sike the view helps to ban a tongue sweeps up sop
my strut stew welts the fan a young sweet blood pops

Ill

Ain't no hesitation
when we love the man

who interrupts the town.
School children familiar

with the family interrupt
school with versions of

lewd and true confusion
involving a hard-to-love

man we come love.
When children belch

my uncle's name
they break in

to hold his nick-
name to their lips

toss it 'cross
the floor as

to keep this
part of me

from me.
I claim I wasn't

close to town nor
to the man I love

and don't know
where they squarely

nail any sense of truth.
When Daddy leaves

the house this late,
it's to go love his brother

who interrupts
the home.

After the 10 o'clock
news the landline

becomes an alarm
and the man we

love, who doesn't
drive, wobbles

unharmed across
Crenshaw's streets.

Curled inside dependency's
teeth who preferred to

eat men. The cops
in the town know

who belongs to who.
The over-courteous

ones detain him until
his brother arrives.

He refuses to drink
the water they give

him and claims the
water is what has

made him ill in
the first place.

A Midnight Cool

I.

I've got a beat in my bones

that I cannot outrun. A

badly battered ode of

bottled bass. Splashing

from bone like beer

from a broken bottle

tapped against the concrete.

II.

The thought of the next

day is often an odd future

to ponder when the lady

twenty years your senior

is eyeing you, wants to

teach you a lesson in the

middle of a crowded floor

as soon as Z.Z. Hill screams,

"Baby don't panic, 'cause I'm

a shadetree mechanic!"

and you learn for the

first time that your youth

offers little advantage over

the motivation from a lady.

Here, the bodies pull in

attraction to a song like

magnets in a room full

of magnets. It is wrapped in

the stingy light of night,

a dark day where, if you're

not timid, you can make the

sun rise in the palm of her hand.

III.

He dances to the chaos for

he has not distinguished

music from noise, nor is he

aware of how sound can

disguise itself as noise, or

other days, even music.

IV.

She obeys desires of the body

needs of the feet and every wish

of the hips, her arms rise in air

like anxious growing trees and

the fingers snap at random

and are limbs in a beat-filled storm

where whiskey snakes through

the air sweet as Glenda's perfume,

in this jukebox-sugar-shack,

pregnant with a beat-filled

kick thrust, heaving pleasure.

v.

Here, the moon has no grip on

the duration of the night, this

party, dark as a healing scab

is inundated with input to skins,

ears, noses, filtering each

thing the valiant mouths of

night will ever remember tasting.

Once They Brought It in the House

cast the brute and iron the pan
a box where the   pies rise in slow
in order to grow in   gold

muscles push dials worn by
time and fade   and memory   a tool
where recipes go   daddy's apron

could cover the bed   his mouth of jokes
they bust the gut   tender as onions
who bow in the mouth   a lake of gravy

a licked off plate   the head   of a pig
who fits   in his pot   has arrived
inside   the hottest mouth   in the house

Soopah Thik

how glance bluff we thick commencement cuh slang lend gut ideas
chow sand snuff see sit cement cent suh hang blend mutt fly deal
wow man shucks he shyt contentment the sang land cut by steals

sow can gruff free it intentional wranglin' strut die meal
vow ran rough be hit we mention a danglin' but why heal
plow an' stuff me wit' resentment fuh stranglin' what i feel

plow an' stuff me wit' resentment fuh stranglin' what i feel
vow ran rough be hit we mention a danglin' but why heal
sow can gruff free it intentional wranglin' strut die meal

wow man shucks he shyt contentment the sang land cut by steals
chow sand snuff see sit cement cent suh hang blend mutt fly deal
how glance bluff we thick commencement cuh slang lend gut ideas

Hulett Street

stop sign to stop sign,
the last bell leaks
sifting the day

to a tune through Hulett street.
wall of yellow buses
parking-lot lit
diesel hangin' in the air
stench like an empty noose
tone for the fight picked by its loser

       we were three blocks
       north of the creek
       below the train tracks

close enough for railcar
rumble to texture our
afternoons. a horn to blow
since we callin' it a song.

down the hall, to the right
up on the boys' bathroom wall
hung a dingy white trough.

we were reservoir dogs, bladder
filled with piss from breakfast,
Brian Merrell flashes a little green

bag while we sported pole-to-pole
lean and lifts of penis, 'till a son,
either end, got pissed on.

hundred-meter men's
burst barefoot on blacktop,
the smoke smelled like sweat

and disfigured laffy taffys. us
husky boys had to watch, or wrestle.

      Koot was a magician, black tire
      melting itself in the asphalt.

he could walk a bike from
stop sign to stop sign, 'bout two
      hundred fifty yards grinnin'
      like a bitch. front wheel, airborne
      spinnin' slow like a ferris wheel.

Koot invented that shit. we were
innovators. gunpowder in a napkin

walloped into the asphalt. the girls
with strawberry Neptunes

growing from their lips – glossy,
like the dope in Bear Parker's eyes –

till those planets popped and flattened
over their wide brown noses.

other girls, fundraising their wrapped
chocolates, pieces of themselves,

songs melting from their mouths
and colored ropes swinging overhead,

> below quick feet, other girls bleeding
> for the first time, oozing what they
> don't know, or what they were

afraid to show Momma so not to be
punished for a thing they'd never

seen. every day, the lesson was to tear
a perfect ring of styrofoam from the rim

of the freeze cup. we were all divas
or vampires constructed by a collage

of after schoolhouse red, a kiss
stenciled with her mother's lipstick,

a fight fixed by a fist fixin' to pierce
the skin and you're just twelve, with

a black eye staring in awe at the girl
you'll never have, April Smith

with the Jheri curl, shirt collar wet,
lips thick as two swollen thumbs
sideways, glistening electric red,

blowing strawberry Jupiters,
walked like she had wheels bolted
under her British Knights, attitude

of the juice of a ginger root, her
skin and speech, chocolates fit for

fundraising, curing sweet teeth
and joneses plunging in
the courses of growing bones.

7th Peered Langwich Arts

boffum cut the rope the phone
boffum snuck a smoke fuh home
   boffum up cuz awoke the domes
boffum trust a cloak the zone

   boffum fuck cuz the yolk the roam
boffum cuz a stroke the loan
   boffum rub just to poke the bone
   boffum love was a joke alone

   boffum love was a joker wrong
   boffum rub just to poke the bone
boffum cuz a stroke the loan
   boffum fuck cuz the yolk the roam

boffum trust a cloak the zone
   boffum up cuz awoke the domes
boffum cut the rope the phone
boffum snuck a smoke fuh home

Two Pit Bulls & a Bone

It is difficult to bark while
the teeth are clinched

so it goes, deep growl
after mean-ass growl

and tug. The oldest holds
her jaw low and doesn't

cease her pull and the mud
slings but not the thing

the dogs won't let go of.
Scraped, inedible and nothing

is left on the bone that
is no bone or for dogs

to chaw on. I ask from my
head amongst the sick

commotion, what could
force me to fight for things

that are not there. How form
might make a difference

in who might fix their fists
to fight for some real shit.

Neither of the dogs authored
the thing but invest their teeth

in the thrash of blood
and ripped up brawn

slush and constant Delta
rainwater. No one wants it

more than dogs and no one but
the dogs will fight. So we let them

mix the mud and blood, the bone
saliva drenched and fractured

and the fight feels closer
to pride than it is to hunger

closer to territory or seniority
than it is the mortality

these bitches go to work in.
And what have the teeth been

after all this time? What drove
this one bitch, to want

the dry bone badder than–
this other bitch did?

Field of View

a field   of summer corn   staked with
tassels   tickling the lowest   air the sky

can claim   a murder of crows   caw and
caution against danger and its   motor of

men   the sky   down here   we name
cerulean   after what we remember first

men promised   wings I pawned at
the corner of   U. S. Route 51   and

Mississippi's Highway 6   in a country store
in Panola County   its name   Cherokee

for cotton   near a river's hurt imitation
of a bigger river   the Anishinaabeg call

Gichi-ziibi   I stare at a   palpable amount
of   theft in my address   I ought to

apologize for   the cameras sittin'   back
above my nose   the registered cerulean

filling the sphere   the lust   at having
been granted   such ancient sky

The Mistaken Identity of Some Verbs

don'tchu love   to open the face   of new fruit don'tchu marvel

at the bright light   on fresh skin   ain'tchu high on somethin'

nobody you love sells   ain'tchu trynna see   where they keep the seeds

ain'tchu hungrier   than you care   to admit   ain'tchu trynna sign

some contract with power   ain'tchu loose   from its tree   ain'tchu just

full   of a lot of ain't   and promise   ain'tchu hopin'   I stop sayin'

ain't ain'tchu hopin'   I stop callin'   yo' name   ain'tcho desire

too old for the feast   ain'tchu eva been beat   ain'tchu eva been

somebody's drum   ain't that tree   too far   for you to reach

ain'tchu   gon' squirm   ain't it missin'   from the news   didn't it

promise you it'd   sing you that song   until it died   didn't you

kill it   ain't this a case   of the mistaken identity of did   didn't you take

your eyes off the prize   didn't you lose   ain'tchu tired   of thinkin'

you won   didn't nothin' ever come   and tell you to stop

didn't you lick   the juice thickenin' down your arm   couldn't we have avoided this   given our past   couldn't we get   nobody

to take notes   couldn't you have heard   it a little bit louder

couldn't   it have not   smelt so phukin' sweet   so new

couldn't you   hear the fists   bangin' hard   at the door

Ode to a Pronoun

it   hung around

      the air

      with wet hair and sweat   it

told us we were

      not in the guts

      of a policed jungle   it

soon ain't gon be no mo' bullets in the gun   it

didn't vote   it

knew what a muthaphuka

      on the porch

      in a suit meant for them   it

wouldn't pull up its pants   it

      studied   it

      danced   it

      thought   it

and won   it

and spoke   it

ran   and

bled   it

ran and   it

is almost time

for these hungry muthaphukas

to eat.

Judith and Holofernes

oil on linen, 120" x 90" by Kehinde Wiley, 2012

in the frame stood all that could be done.
a dash of blood on a long and ready blade.
a justice this particular day made late. one
head without a body, hanging from the other
body. a sign to be read, not spoken. a wish
to be wished and not had. the problem is
it's already done and up on the wall and
although it is there, happened and recorded,
its broken chronology won't be mentioned.

I am stuck in the contrast of garden and
grave. all bloom all wither, all pattern and its
sore disruption. every aunt I have known
nails set to a dazzle wears the sweet remix
of Judith. blushed to balance out the gore.
the chain-linked wallpaper stares back at
what seemed to be the only feeling left.
a lie stuffed under our beds for our good.
who's the poor tyrant in our own Bethulia?
who's lured us into this hunting, spooked
us into such a calamitous marriage?

Land of the Plea Home of the Grave

hung mines who sinnin' tales go wrong who bit the trustful zoo the wire
hum rhymes choose billin' jails crow roams choose spit the custard spew the liar
scum swine blew shrillin' scales throw on blue shyt a buzzard two a mire

gun times shoes spinnin' trails low moan shoe fit the mustard drew the ire
punch lines due grinnin' bails tow home due pitch fuh lussful coup a choir
sometimes you been in hell so long you get accustomed to the fire

sometimes you been in hell so long you get accustomed to the fire
punch lines due grinnin' bails tow home due pitch fuh lussful coup a choir
gun times shoes spinnin' trails low moan shoe fit the mustard drew the ire

scum swine blew shrillin' scales throw on blue shyt a buzzard two a mire
hum rhymes choose billin' jails crow roams choose spit the custard spew the liar
hung mines who sinnin' tales go wrong who bit the trustful zoo the wire

The Haunting

a chance to aid   his erections comes
true in the street   a call about thieves

slide over all the   other rovers
a bad song agitates wild   on the siren

tires screech anxious   licking the asphalt
a soda can still on the curb   guns are

drawn in the paws of the   haunted
who think they've seen the   ghost they

know they deserve   a lie about what
was seen is printed on paper   apologies

mumbled at the   press conference a bag
of pennies   sent to the family's home

I am drowned by   the leftovers of
myself on   these   streets

Who Can Govern Themselves Out of Governance?

if I could be somewhere
I wasn't I would be there

or I would have already
paid that place some

cold and charitable visit.
if you knew how wealthy

I wasn't you would run.
I cannot remember

what I was before I tried
to become what I thought

I could in light of the
dark that swallowed me.

the story of how I thought
I had not been pure and

had not been enough. how
I was not there though I

had been but was gone
after what I did not

know I did not need
came. how do you fix

that which the house
has no tools to fix?

where is the resolve as
bright as the wet face

of a child, the sight of the
rigid origin of the break?

A Reason to Git Back

bush hogs ova feet drain drawls
gushin' dogs go fuh treats rain falled
slushin' frogs sober Sweet James Jones

brushin' fogs off undah peak nightfall
rushin' hogs off up on meek freak hall
pushin' flogs off us in the reekin' white zones

pushin' flogs off us in the reekin' white zones
rushin' hogs off up on meek freak hall
brushin' fogs off undah peak nightfall

slushin' frogs sober Sweet James Jones
gushin' dogs go fuh treats rain falled
bush hogs ova feet drain drawls

Fuh da Summa

I'm docked at a lake that
the people don't attend.

Machete on my hip to
make a devil cough up

blood   dust and light.
Hungry for ruins of

an afternoon of anything
wild and willing to stick

its neck through the roof
of the leftover lake. I'm

docked at a lake that ain't
got no river   in a field that

ain't   got no fence   under a
sun that ain't   never heard

of mercy. I'm docked at the
edge of an unfortunate dinner

next to a wet knot of Cotton-
mouths   too big to see.

ACKNOWLEDGEMENTS

My thanks and gratitude go out to the editors of the following journals, magazines and anthologies where many of these poems first appeared, some in earlier versions: *The Academy of American Poets Poem-a-Day digital poetry series, 128 Lit Magazine, Obsidian Literature & Arts in the African Diaspora, The Yale Review, Los Angeles Review of Books Quarterly Journal, Manual: a journal about art and its making, Virginia Quarterly Review, Ecotone, Boston Review, Callaloo: A Journal of African Diaspora Arts and Letters, Voluble: A Channel of Los Angeles Review of Books, Mississippi Review, Pinwheel, Lumberyard Magazine, PLUCK! The Journal of Affrilachian Arts and Culture,* and *"What Things Cost: An Anthology for the People"* from the The University Press of Kentucky.

My deepest and most unbridled appreciation to the following institutions who've provided time, collaboration, support and resources for my work: Spalding University's MFA in Writing, Callaloo's Creative Writing Workshop and Conference, New York University's MFA in Creative Writing, Poets & Writers, Vermont Studio Center, The Fine Arts Work Center in Provincetown, The Bread Loaf Writer's Conference, Naropa University Summer Writing Program, The University of Rhode Island, The St. Botolph Club Foundation, Boise City Department of Arts & History and The James Castle House Residency, The Elizabeth Murray Artist Residency, and Wesleyan University.

To my brother Lanier, you've been there since they didn't let me walk on at Northwest. You've seen every snag in the process thus far and always supported and sometimes helped steer this thing toward where my heart was, Route 1, Box 22. To Jackson, Mississippi, and the artists who were there from the jump and the incubator that was Seven*Studioz, you have my love! To Ezra Brown, Donyale Walls, Kenneth Stiggers, Norma Michael, Midget, Try One, Skip Coon, Kanika Welch, Amanda Furdge, Devin Estes, Urban Raw (Rest in Peace & Power), Felandus Thames, Jackson Harlem, Kerry and Kelly Nash (The Vibe Controllers), Talibah Mawusi, Thabi Moyo, Carlton Turner, Mary Sneed, Kenyatta Pratt, Alexius Rashod, Lorenzo Gayden, Angelica

Geter, Ken Patterson, Matthew Simmons, D. J. Phingaprint and D. J. Venom and to those whose names are buried deep in my heart, I can't thank you all enough. More love and gratitude to my co-conspirators or otherwise fellows and folks in the word and in life: Elizabeth L. Butler, Jeremy Michael Clark, Lillian Yvonne-Bertram, Makalani Bandele, Jayson P. Smith, S*an D. Henry-Smith, Desiree C. Bailey, Marwa Helal, Jonah Mixon-Webster, Rodrick Minor, Sanderia Faye, Tiana Clark, CL Young, Ross Gay, Chris Mattingly, Patrick Rosal, Alysia Harris, Emma Hine, Nabila Lovelace, Diannely Antigua, Monica Sok, Sable Elyse Smith, Ashley M. Jones, the 2012 and 2013 Callaloo Creative Writing Workshops and the 2016 Conversation Literary Festival fellows. I also extend my deep appreciation for the teachers and mentors who've met and led me with kindness and love, helping shape my relationship with language: the late Iris Marie Leggette, Ida Allen, C. Leigh McInnis, Noel Didla, Gregory Pardlo, Vievee Francis, Randall Horton, Charles Henry Rowell, Kathleen Driskell, Greg Pape, Maureen Morehead, Jeanie Thompson, Major Jackson, Sharon Olds, Yusef Komunyakaa, Rachel Zucker, Eileen Myles, Peter Covino, Martha Elena Rojas and Christine Mok. A quarry of thanks to the good people at Four Way Books for their belief, knowledge and expertise in transforming this manuscript into a book. To Martha Rhodes, Ryan Murphy, and Nancy Koerbel, Thank you! I owe more gratitude than I can afford to francine j. harris and John Murillo for their kindness, time, listening and seeing. To Fred Moten, your whole approach to the word is a blessing. Thank you for the fellowship. Your generosity has been no small gesture.

And for you, dear reader, I am forever grateful to get to share this language with you.

A. H. Jerriod Avant was born and raised in Longtown, Mississippi. His first book, *Muscadine*, is forthcoming from Four Way Books (September, 2023). A graduate of Jackson State University, Jerriod has earned MFA degrees from Spalding University and New York University. He's received scholarships from the Breadloaf Writer's Conference and Naropa University's Summer Writing Program. A former resident at the James Castle House and Vermont Studio Center, Jerriod has received two winter fellowships from the Fine Arts Work Center in Provincetown and an emerging artist grant from the St. Botolph Club Foundation. His work has appeared in the *Boston Review, Pinwheel, Callaloo, Virginia Quarterly Review, Obsidian, The Yale Review*, and other journals. He's currently a Ph.D. English candidate (Spring 2023) at the University of Rhode Island and a Teaching Fellow in English at Wesleyan University.

PUBLICATION OF THIS BOOK WAS MADE POSSIBLE BY GRANTS AND
DONATIONS. WE ARE ALSO GRATEFUL TO THOSE INDIVIDUALS WHO
PARTICIPATED IN OUR BUILD A BOOK PROGRAM. THEY ARE:

Anonymous (14), Robert Abrams, Michael Ansara, Kathy Aponick, Jean Ball,
Sally Ball, Clayre Benzadon, Adrian Blevins, Laurel Blossom, Adam Bohannon,
Betsy Bonner, Patricia Bottomley, Lee Briccetti, Joel Brouwer, Susan Buttenwieser,
Anthony Cappo, Paul and Brandy Carlson, Dan Clarke, Mark Conway, Elinor
Cramer, Kwame Dawes, Michael Anna de Armas, John Del Peschio, Brian Komei
Dempster, Rosalynde Vas Dias, Patrick Donnelly, Lynn Emanuel, Blas Falconer,
Jennifer Franklin, John Gallaher, Reginald Gibbons, Rebecca Kaiser Gibson,
Dorothy Tapper Goldman, Julia Guez, Naomi Guttman and Jonathan Mead,
Forrest Hamer, Luke Hankins, Yona Harvey, KT Herr, Karen Hildebrand, Carlie
Hoffman, Glenna Horton, Thomas and Autumn Howard, Catherine Hoyser,
Elizabeth Jackson, Linda Susan Jackson, Jessica Jacobs and Nickole Brown,
Lee Jenkins, Elizabeth Kanell, Nancy Kassell, Maeve Kinkead, Victoria Korth,
Brett Lauer and Gretchen Scott, Howard Levy, Owen Lewis and Susan Ennis,
Margaree Little, Sara London and Dean Albarelli, Tariq Luthun, Myra Malkin,
Louise Mathias, Victoria McCoy, Lupe Mendez, Michael and Nancy Murphy,
Kimberly Nunes, Susan Okie and Walter Weiss, Cathy McArthur Palermo,
Veronica Patterson, Jill Pearlman, Marcia and Chris Pelletiere, Sam Perkins, Susan
Peters and Morgan Driscoll, Maya Pindyck, Megan Pinto, Kevin Prufer, Martha
Rhodes & Jean Brunel, Paula Rhodes, Louise Riemer, Peter and Jill Schireson,
Rob Schlegel, Yoana Setzer, Soraya Shalforoosh, Mary Slechta, Diane Souvaine,
Barbara Spark, Catherine Stearns, Jacob Strautmann, Yerra Sugarman, Arthur Sze
& Carol Moldaw, Marjorie and Lew Tesser, Dorothy Thomas, Rushi Vyas, Martha
Webster and Robert Fuentes, Rachel Weintraub and Allston James, Abby Wender
and Rohan Weerasinghe, Monica Youn.